BRING YOUR MICCC

MONEY

Also by Diamond Wilson

Books
THE QUEST FOR THE QUEEN
Book One: The Caves of Qumran
Book Two: Dangers in the Desert

LITTLE WORDS, BIG IDEAS
Book One: Going Bananas
Book Two: Antithesis' Labyrinth

Videos
Thinking Forward For Your Future Self: Establishing Your i+1 | Diamond Wilson | TEDxPlano

BRING YOUR MICCC

MONEY

DIAMOND WILSON

If you purchased this book without a cover, you should be aware that this book is stolen property. It was reported as "unsold and destroyed" to the publisher, and neither the author nor the publisher has received any payment for this "stripped" book.

In no way is the content in this book meant to provide counsel, either emotional, psychological, or financial, to the reader. The information contained in this book is opinion only, and is based on a unique perspective and experience. The author and contributors are not professional financial managers nor crisis counselors, and are not certified to give legal, psychological, or financial advice. All decisions that are made and acted upon by the readers regarding their well-being are their responsibility alone.

Copyright © 2018 by Diamond Wilson

All rights reserved. Published by LonnaDee Press. No part of this book may be reproduced or transmitted in any form or by any means, electronic or mechanical, including printing, photocopying, recording, or by any information storage and retrieval system, without written permission from the publisher.

First LonnaDee Press paperback edition, 2018
Printed in the United States of America
ISBN: 978-0989859400

Hyper-Spelling done by Mark Schultz at wordrefiner.com

Cover art by Vanessa Flores
Cover photo by Shawn O'Connell

Visit: diamondwilson.com

*To Jonathan. For the creative mind,
there are no walls that cannot be breached.*

CONTENTS

Introduction	*i*
Why Do We Need Money?	*1*
What Is Money?	*3*
So, What's Up With Minimum Wage Jobs?	*6*
How Do I Get Money?	*14*
Letters of Recommendation	*16*
Let's Talk About the Interview	*20*
When Is It Enough?	*31*
Let's Talk About Budgets	*34*
Let's Crush Some of Your Best Arguments. Bring 'em On.	*38*
Some Special Situations Where It's Crucial to Have Your Finances Under Control	*48*
Bonus Warnings: Parties and Dates	*53*
Bonus Warnings: Roommates and Credit	*56*
The Skinny on Student Loans	*63*
What if I've Already Ruined my Chances?	*67*

INTRODUCTION

This book is the first in the series of the *Bring Your MICCC* collection. The seed for this book was planted when I was a Sophomore at Montana State University. I was working three jobs, studying three languages, and trying to fashion a woman out of the awkward girl I was at the time. Early mornings slinging espresso bled into late nights closing the restaurant, with a full load of classes and an afternoon job in between.

One night, I was driving home from work at 2 a.m. in the snow. I was freezing, tired, and had to open the coffee shop at 5:00 a.m.—in only three hours. My feet were tired from waiting tables all night, and I sat in my car for a moment longer than necessary when I parked outside my apartment, dreading the stairs.

Making it all on my own was hard. Very hard. And it wasn't just hard for me. Some friends had maxed out their credit cards buying groceries, while others had a strict budget of $70 to spend on food the whole month. College tuition was expensive (it's even more expensive now), and spring break trips were out of the question for people like me and my friends.

That night, as I sat in my car, I slipped twenty-three dollars from my restaurant job tips and put them in my other pocket. I committed to saving a twenty-dollar bill and all my ones every shift I worked at the restaurant. It was hard. It was hard not to steal from myself to indulge in a plate of hot pasta or a latte and a scone from my favorite places near the campus. And, to be honest, I didn't always have the discipline to follow through.

I had student loans coming out of college. They were even worse after graduate school. And I hadn't really developed strong money habits yet, but the seed was planted. I knew firsthand just how important money was. Not just having it, but also the ability to make it in a pinch and to make it go a long way when I had to.

This fuzzy inkling of money as a foundation point to success and to adulting is really what shaped my establishing the course, and now the book series, *Bring Your MICCC*. I realized that if someone didn't have control over their own money, and a way to earn it, they were powerless and completely at the mercy of whomever held their financial strings.

Over time, and through countless discussions with friends, mentors, peers, and people who had overcome seemingly impossible odds, the rest of the concepts fleshed themselves out and made an appearance in this course.

Erika Vargas Estrada, founder of EM Vargas Consulting, played a key role in many of the concepts in this book. We had the opportunity to present "Bring Your MICCC" together at two conferences in Dallas, Texas, and Erika is responsible for the "C" of curiosity! She also introduced me to the Amy Cuddy TED Talk, which is recommended in this book.

Bring Your MICCC is all about setting yourself up for success; it's about having a secure platform that will help you excel.

The series is called "*Bring Your MICCC*" because after we finish school (where everyone is practically begging us to participate), the world turns out to be pretty uninterested in our thoughts, opinions, and expectations. Instead, there is much more value placed upon what we can do with what we know, and how we can add value to the world around us—practical value, not potential value.

For those of you just starting out, your MICCC—Money, Image, Crew, Curiosity, and Creativity—is going to transmit your voice loudly and clearly. Your MICCC will help you do this in a way that will encourage others to take note of you and listen to what you have to say; after all, your track record shows you're a doer, not just a talker.

I hope you read, learn, live, love, strive, struggle, and evolve!

MONEY

Money is a tricky subject to talk about. Sometimes it's uncomfortable. Sometimes it's downright stressful. Money can cause couples to fight, friends to resent each other, and weaken the close bond between families. It's necessary for survival, and, if you've been working and trying to hold your own, you know how quickly it gets away from you—and rarely because you got to do something fun with it.

Life is full of emergencies, and generally these emergencies require cash, time, and energy. (Like the average person has any of those things to spare!)

In this chapter, I'm going to help you see the importance of money while (hopefully) not stressing you out about something most of the world doesn't have enough of. I'm also going to help you prepare so that money doesn't have to become your master, because it's a cruel one.

> "MONEY IS A TERRIBLE MASTER, BUT AN EXCELLENT SERVANT."
> -P.T. BARNUM

Why Do We Need Money?

Yes, I just asked that question. While it seems basic, I want you to take a moment and think about why *you* need money. Maybe you need it to pay rent or put gas in your car. Maybe it's for food, clothes, or going to the movies with friends.

Maybe you want to go to Asia so you can say you've been halfway around the world, or maybe you want to do something nice for your girlfriend or boyfriend for Valentine's Day.

When it boils down to it, we all have needs and wants. Money helps satisfy both. Here is the big difference between needs and wants: not having a need met will result in damage or harm. Not having a want met might result in disappointment.

Think about it...

Can you distinguish your needs from your wants? How are you going to prioritize your money?

Needs	Wants
_____	_____
_____	_____
_____	_____
_____	_____
_____	_____

What Is Money?

Merriam-Webster defines money as: "something generally accepted as a medium of exchange, a measure of value, or a means of payment."

I want us to particularly focus on a **measure of value** as it relates to work. Ultimately, we don't get paid for showing up to work, or having a job. We get paid because we are providing value to the business or the person who employs us. The amount you get paid is directly correlated to the amount of value you add to your employer. If you want more money, you will have to find a way to increase your value and make sure your employer is a aware of such an increase.

GROUP DISCUSSION

- Why do people get paid overtime? How is that linked to measure of value?
- Why do you think minimum wage jobs don't pay very much?
- What are some skills you can learn at a minimum wage job that will help add value to you as an employee? How can this help you get paid more in the future at this company or at your next job?

Personal Questions

- What are some ways I add value? (these can be intangibles, such as your positive attitude, consistency, work ethic, etc.)
- What are some ways my manager (boss, parent, sibling, etc.) adds value, and what can I learn from them?
- Who is my ideal co-worker, based on my strengths and weaknesses? What are some values this pretend person has?

This space is here so you can doodle if you want to when you are done. You're welcome.

Money, in modern days, comes in the form of cash, card, or check. Many of us deposit it into our bank account, spend it at the store, or spend it online all without ever seeing a single penny.

But that doesn't make it less valuable. It's not about what we see; it's what we can do with it and what it represents.

Money is

a **representation**

of the **value**

you add to your company

by doing

a certain amount

of **work**.

Skilled jobs, such as coding, construction, cosmetology, mechanics, programming, plumbing, etc. pay more than minimum wage because:

1. These jobs require credentials, so there is more demand than supply.

2. They add great **value**, oftentimes value that is connected with making your life easier, more pleasant, and more productive.

> *Those blanks are for you to fill in!*
>
> **Some specialty jobs that add great value**
>
> construction
> **coding**
> plumbing   programming
>   mechanics
>   cosmetology
> _____   _____
>
> _____   _____

So, What's Up With Minimum Wage Jobs?

This doesn't mean that minimum wage jobs aren't necessary; they are, and there are jobs available in almost every field! The **difference** between a minimum wage job and a specialty job is in the training, education, and certifications they require. Most people, without specialized training, can learn to do a minimum wage job fairly well, fairly quickly.

As we acquire skills in a minimum wage job, it prepares us to take on something a little more challenging.

To make sure that you are on the lookout for skills you can (and should!) learn at a minimum wage job, I've polled some successful professionals, educators, and managers who've worked their way up from the bottom to see what they think.

Hint

Keep a running document of all your job activities; it's easy to forget everything you do when asking for a raise or building a résumé.

-Erin Huebener

Name:

Andy Brown

Profession:

Author and Internet Radio Show Host

What he looks for when he is hiring someone:

Someone who is energetic, consistent, willing to learn, and who has a team mind-set

What he thinks people can learn from minimum wage jobs:

First, tell yourself "This is not enough." Define what you need to reach for. Ask yourself what made you want to work at that job and what draws the customers there. Convenience? Technology? Efficiency?

Think about ways you can make your job easier; think of ways to simplify the approach.

Constantly consider how you can modify the external content based on your unique perspective of the internal operations. Think of a way to sell the improvement.

Name:

Caroline Bickford

Profession:

Hairstylist

What she appreciates in a co-worker:

She enjoyes working with people who are humble, who have the ability to learn from their job, listen, and be teachable. She appreciates it when management is respectful, leads by example, and has honest and clear communication.

Why she chose to study a trade first on her path to becoming a counselor:

"I came from a family that didn't have much money and my dad encouraged us to find a trade to send ourselves to college, since trade schools are not that expensive.

I knew hairstyling was the first step for me... I worked for a year and a half before starting on my Associate Degree.

I'm in college, but I'm trying to be smart with finances. I took out some student loans already, but now I'm taking it slow. I won't take out any more loans until I'm working on my Master's Degree."

Name:

Robert Jones

Profession:

Teacher and Coach

What he looks for when he is assigning leadership roles:

When I'm looking to place a player in a leadership role, I'm looking for someone who demonstrates servant-type leadership, someone who is willing to lead by example and who has high character both on and off the field, in the classroom, and at home.

What he thinks people can learn from minimum wage jobs:

Experience at a minimum wage job teaches you the discipline of being on time and being accountable for your actions.

These types of jobs provide the opportunity for you to learn to listen, take directives, and turn those directives into actions that in turn provide a positive influence in your life.

As you develop these skills, along with a work ethic, you become a worker that technology, no matter how great, cannot replace.

A WORD OF WARNING!

Many young people (and college graduates!) aren't willing to start at the "bottom of the totem pole." They don't want to take out the trash, clean kennels, or work at a fast food restaurant.

It's a common human problem to think "I'm too good for *THAT*." Instead of taking it humbly and working their way up, they want to start off somewhere in the middle. Somewhere that's not cleaning the toilet, washing the dishes, or doing monotonous work.

REALITY CHECK!

Until you've done those things, and proven that you can do them well, **you aren't as qualified as someone else who has done them**! So, suck it up, get an entry level job, and evaluate yourself. Ask others to evaluate you. Ask a mentor what you can do to improve, or what skills and character traits you should work on so that you are eligible and desirable for the next best position.

PERSONAL EXAMPLE:
How Sweet and Sour Chicken Changed My Life

When I was fifteen years old, I got a job at the Wok in Bozeman, Montana. I worked at this Chinese food restaurant under the close supervision and mentorship of the owner, a gentleman named Herman.

I was a hostess, and I made minimum wage plus tips from carryout orders.

My duties included greeting and seating guests, answering the phone, taking to-go orders, packing those orders when the kitchen had processed them, and taking payments both over the phone and in person.

We didn't have a staff member to deliver the food. Instead, we contracted a delivery service to handle those orders for us. I'll never forget a particular busy Friday night, or the hard lesson that I had to learn that left a lump in my throat and tears in my eyes.

It all began with Sweet and Sour Chicken. It was a simple to-go order, but the person on the line had been on hold for at least three minutes (which feels like an eternity when you are on hold JUST to order Sweet and Sour Chicken). The entire entry way was flooded with people, and even the grinning Buddha statue that was next to the restroom was sick of having his belly rubbed by so many people at once.

I rushed away from the register as soon as I had half a chance, and thanked the person for holding. I took the order and the credit card payment over the phone.

"That will be ready in about twenty minutes," I said cheerfully.

"Oh, I wanted that for delivery."

It was all I could do to not roll my eyes.

This was going to take me three minutes longer than I had planned. I wrote down the address, upped the expected delivery time to forty-five minutes, and hung up. I didn't write down the phone number, *because I was too busy*.

I called the delivery service.

"It's going to be a long one," the driver told me. "An hour and fifteen minutes before I can get it there."

"Okay," I said. "I quoted them 45."

"Call 'em back and let 'em know it's going to be longer," he told me. I looked out into the dark night and could see the blizzard.

I couldn't call them back. I crossed my fingers and hoped they were understanding, and got back to work dealing with the line. Crazy, but Chinese restaurants always seem to be busy in the worst weather when you'd think everyone would order pizza and stay home.

Fifty minutes went by like a snap, and suddenly, my to-go order was up and ready to pack. I grabbed a small container and filled it with white rice out of the giant pot in the back. I grabbed a bag with soy sauce, mustard, and fortune cookies, and stapled the paper bag shut.

The delivery service got the bag, delivered it to the address, and finally, the rush started to quiet down. It was only then I saw a small box of sweet and sour sauce going stale in the heated kitchen window. My heart sank. I'd forgotten to put it in the bag.

I fessed up. I caught Herman by the arm, and told him what had happened. Just then, the phone rang. It was a very dissatisfied customer. Their order had arrive half-an-hour late, and without any sauce.

"I'm so sorry," Herman said. "I'm sending another one to you right now."

He went back to the kitchen and told the cooks to get another one on the fly. Then, he came to speak with me.

Herman and I had a great relationship. He was teaching me Mandarin during slow times, gave me a gift on Christmas, and had even promoted me to Assistant Manager when I was only fifteen, with my main responsibility being to close down the till at the end of the night. I want to clarify my respect for him and my desire to please my employer so you know how I felt when we had "the conversation."

"Diamond," he told me, "we have to pay four dollars every time we send out a delivery. Tonight, we sent out two Sweet and Sour Chickens in two deliveries, and we aren't going to get paid for that at all because we are trying to keep our customer. That's twenty dollars lost because of one mistake. I can't afford to pay for you and your mistakes."

I apologized, and offered to pay for my mistake. He didn't take my money. Instead, he taught me a valuable lesson: **if you don't have time to do it right, you most certainly can't afford to do it twice.**

On that snowy winter night, Herman taught me how I could upgrade my value as a worker by double-checking my finished product, and making sure everything was correct, every time. While working at the Wok, I never again sent out an incorrect order.

> I attribute some of my greatest work-ethic skills to the things I learned from working alongside Herman. He was my first workplace mentor, and I tried to learn as much as I could from him in the year and a half I worked there.
>
> When I graduated from high school, he gave me a red envelope with a one-hundred dollar bill stuffed inside. It was the most money anyone had ever given me, but that money couldn't compare to the countless lessons he taught me.

How Do I Get Money?

When you're just starting out, earning money is hard. Even when you want to work and you're willing to work, someone has to take a chance on you.

An employer has a lot of things to consider when he or she hires you. Employers have to think about safety (they pay for accidents that happen on the job), reputation, quality of work, speed and total output that you accomplish in a given

Circle those that apply to you!

FAST LEARNER FRIENDLY
RELIABLE
HIGH ACHIEVER
PUNCTUAL
GOAL-SETTER BILINGUAL

Why should they hire ME?

STRONG MOTIVATOR
FUN TO WORK WITH
COACHABLE THOROUGH
CONSISTENT
TEAM-PLAYER EXPERIENCE
POSITIVE ATTITUDE

amount of time, and the cost of paying you. If the benefits don't undoubtedly outweigh the costs, your would-be employer is going to move on to the next application in the stack.

The good news is, now that you know some of the concerns a potential employer might have, you can begin to reassure the person who does the hiring by putting together a portfolio.

Grades, letters of recommendation, and any experience you have in school groups, church groups, sports, and community groups will help paint a picture to your future employer of the type of *person* you are, and therefore the type of *employee* you are likely to be.

Personal Questions

- Who can I get letters of recommendation from?
- What if I don't have any experience in any clubs, organizations, or groups? What are three groups I can join to start building that experience?

Letters of Recommendation

There are some things *you* can do to help your letter stand out. Most young people (at the last minute, before a job or scholarship application is due) say "Hey, can you write me a letter of recommendation? I know it's last minute, but my stuff is all due tomorrow." Don't be that person. Imagine the type of letter you are going to get:

> To Whom it May Concern:
>
> I've had _____ in my class for two semesters. S/he is an all-around likable person, but could use a little bit of time management skills and needs work on the concept of "beginning with the end in mind."

And so on.

Instead, imagine you say to your teacher, coach, or youth leader: "I am applying for a position for a summer job at (this specific location). According to the job description, they are looking for someone who is (trustworthy, punctual, has graphic skills, is bilingual, etc). Since I have proven to be (honest, precise, a good time manager, etc) in your class/group/team, I thought you would be a great person to ask for a letter of recommendation. I'd like to turn in that application at the beginning of next week. Would you be able to help me?"

Now, your mentor knows exactly what type of position they are recommending you for, when you are planning to take the job, and what specific qualities they can highlight based on the particular position (scholarship, internship, etc.) for which you are applying. Not only does this make them think even more highly of you, but it gets *you* a better recommendation than just the simple form letter.

Here are some real examples of letters of recommendation:

> To the Admissions Staff at Dr. Emmett J. Conrad Global Collegiate Academy,
>
> It is my privilege to introduce R—, a respectful young man with a sweet disposition and pleasant attitude. I have had the opportunity to work with R— over the course of the past two school years, and I have seen him mature and take ownership of his responsibilities.
>
> One of R—'s greatest strengths is the way he interacts with his peers. He is likable, friendly, and always positive. He is a good team member and knows how to work well with others in the classroom.
>
> R— is also very giving and encouraging. I have seen him help others with their work, explaining concepts and showing great patience. He is reliable and responsible and can be counted on to make up missing work without being reminded.
>
> I recommend R— as a student at Dr. Emmett J. Conrad Global Collegiate Academy and believe he will contribute to both the community and classroom environments.
>
> If you have any questions, please feel free to contact me.
>
> Sincerely,

To the Admissions Staff at Booker T. Washington High School,

It is my privilege to introduce J—, a lovely young lady full of spark, wit, and enthusiasm. I have had the opportunity to work with J— over the course of the past two school years, and I have continued to be impressed with her consistent attitude, work ethic, and the overall glow she brings into any room she enters.

While J— is an incredibly talented young lady, her strengths go far beyond traditional academics. She is very encouraging, makes others feel included, and has a wonderful way of fostering friendly interactions among diverse populations. She is helpful, creative, and truly a joy to work with and to have as a student.

J— is also a very creative thinker. I personally appreciate that she is always up for a challenge, and that she consistently thinks outside of the box. I have been her language teacher for the past two years, and she is one student who regularly pushes the bounds of her own comfort level to go above and beyond in her higher-level thinking.

I can always count on J— to be the leader in the group, to help with a smile, and to enrich the group she is placed in, no matter who that includes. She is a person who is lit from within and who maintains her joyful perspective, in spite of external circumstances.

I would highly recommend J— as a student at Booker T. Washington High School and believe she will be a great contributor to the environment, the talent, and the excellence of this institution.

If you have any questions, please feel free to contact me.

Sincerely,

What You Want Your Letter to Say

To Whom It May Concern:

It is my privilege to introduce _____(name)_____, a young ____(man/lady)____ who demonstrates ____(character trait)____. In the time that I have known ____(name)____, I have continued to be impressed with ____(some awesome things you do)____.

While ____(name)____ is incredibly talented in ____(something you do)____ his/her strengths continue into ____(something else you like)____. S/he is very ____(descriptive adjective)____ and has a wonderful way of ____(something you do that raises others up)____. S/he is also ____(amazing at the following things)____.

One of ____(name's)____ greatest qualities is his/her ability to ____(something you do regularly)____. He/she is able to ____(a skill)____, and s/he is adept at ____(another skill)____.

I would highly recommend ____(name)____ as a ____(title)____ at ____(institution name/company)____, and believe s/he will be a great contributor to the ____(community, environment, vibe, academic standards, etc.)____ of this institution.

If you have any questions, please feel free to contact me.

Sincerely,

_____
(name of ideal recommender)

Let's Talk About the Interview

So now that you have been involved in clubs, groups, teams, and volunteer organizations and have given a mentor plenty of time to write you a great letter (and some ideas of what to focus on), it's time to think about how you are going to present yourself in the interview.

> **FREE ADVICE**
>
> Listen attentively.
> Nod when appropriate.
> Smile, or maintain a pleasant look on your face.

Success Story: The Power of Mental Preparation

Charles Duhigg, in his book *Smarter Faster Better*, makes excellent use of the following story to demonstrate the importance of mental preparation. It is the story of QANTAS flight 32, a plane carrying 440 passengers plus an extended flight crew, and the man in charge who, along with his team of top senior pilots, saved it from crashing.

What happened on the flight is astounding. Stellar communication, exceptional teamwork, a dash of luck, and (most importantly, pertaining to our current discussion) mental preparation.

The flight was supposed to go from Singapore to Sydney, an eight-hour trip one way. That flight never reached its destination. Instead, the plane started falling apart over Indonesia, losing its engine, its logo, and other pieces of shrapnel over a town called Batam. (These details come from an article by Tony J. Hughes. If you'd like to read his article, check the back of the book under the Bibliography section.) It was, in fact, a plane destined to fall out of the sky. It had mechanical issues that no one knew about before it even took off. Were it not for the exceptional folks flying the plane that day, this could have been a fatal tragedy.

Before the flight ever took off, Captain Richard Champion de Crespigny made sure his crew was mentally prepared for the worst, even though the chances for the flight crashing were one in millions.

WHAT WOULD YOU DO IF...

Captain de Crespigny practiced with his copilots, running the crew through hypothetical situations. He asked them what they would do first if there was an engine failure, something that he asked before every flight.

As a group, they discussed each person's particular roles in case of emergency. Captain de Crespigny even encouraged that there be a nay-sayer in the group—someone whose particular job was to make sure they didn't fall into group-think. (Check out *Smarter Faster Better* to read more about this; there are lots of excellent examples in Duhigg's book.)

When the flight was going down, Captain de Crespigny did a few very important things. He allowed his decision to be overturned by other members of his crew. He drew on past experience. He used his imagination when the computer system was no longer an option.

That was the difference between crashing the plane and landing it. When Captain de Crespigny visualized the plane as it was, with the parts of it that were working, and formulated a landable model based on that, he was able to get feedback from his copilots and land the plane on a runway with only one hundred meters to spare.

They landed back in Singapore.

Right now, the kinds of mental paradigms you create and the types of scenarios you practice might not be as intense as safely landing a split-bellied plane. But imagining, practicing possible outcomes, and visualizing your way to solutions is a great skill for all situations in which you find yourself.

Here are some situations where young people have created mental paradigms that have served them very well:
- A flight alone with one or more changes in unfamiliar airports
- An awkward conversation with a parent

- Asking someone out on a date
- Preparing for getting called on (or called out) in class
- Preparing for an emergency, such as getting held up at a gas station
- Reporting someone for sexual harassment
- Talking with a boss, teacher, coach, or someone in authority about needs you have that you don't feel are being met
- Giving a speech or presentation

RANK IN ORDER OF IMPORTANCE TO YOU WHEN IT COMES TO VISUALIZATION: THERE IS NO RIGHT ANSWER

_____What to say

_____What the environment feels like

_____What smells are in the air

_____What happened just a few moments ago

_____The other person's body language

_____What are some sounds, and what do they mean

_____Calling on similar past experiences to guide you

HOW WOULD YOU PREPARE FOR THE FOLLOWING SCENARIOS? PICK ONE, OR DO MULTIPLES:

1. Your parent plans to introduce their new significant other to you over dinner
2. You're going to buy a car, and want to negotiate the best possible price
3. Your car breaks down or gets a flat tire in a bad neighborhood, and your phone is dead

_____
_____
_____
_____
_____
_____
_____

See how having a mental paradigm for each of these situations pushes you a little bit? Isn't it better to think about these things now rather than when you are in a threatening or uncomfortable situation?

Interview Checklist

- Bring your ID, social security card, and birth certificate (or passport)—if you are not a U.S. citizen, also bring your Green Card or Work Permit.
- Do your research! Know about the company, visit the webpage, follow them on social media, and look at any images available online to get a feel for the space, and the dress of the people who work there. (Hint, they got the job.)
- Dress neatly, but not too flashy.
- Make sure you are clean, and give yourself plenty of time to get ready. Don't rush after school or a workout; give yourself some cushion time.
- Don't overdo the perfume or cologne. Fresh and clean is your best bet.
- If you must wait, don't look down at your phone! Keep your head held high, and maybe revisit some of the questions you want to ask. Also, watch this TED talk: https://www.ted.com/talks/amy_cuddy_your_body_language_shapes_who_you_are

- Know the <u>name of your interviewer</u>, if at all possible, and make sure to use it during the interview.
- ALWAYS stand up to shake someone's hand. (This is true at dinners, coffee shops, any place where you are being introduced to someone). Use a firm—but not crushing—handshake, smile, and look the person in the eyes. Repeat their name, and say something pleasant, such as "Nice to meet you!"
- Walk with <u>confidence</u>. Shoulders back, head held high, a smile on your face. Walk at a mid-slow pace, and if you are wearing high heels to the interview, make sure they are comfortable and that you've practiced walking on multiple types of flooring. Also, consider appropriate footwear for the occasion. You might not want to wear heels when you know there will be an outdoor "tour of the grounds."
- Listen carefully; pay attention to what your interviewer is talking about.
- Think of questions you can ask that are relevant to the interviewer/organization, or that have to do with the position, job, duties, or general purpose of the company.
- Be prepared to <u>answer questions</u>! That's what the interview is all about. "I don't know," or "I'm not really sure," are NOT answers that are going to get you any job. If you need a moment to think about it, take it. Go ahead and say: "That's a great question. I'd like a moment to think about how I'd handle that (or what I'd do, the best way to deal with that situation, etc)." Then answer the question concisely and clearly, or say, "You know, I think I need to look up some more information in order to be able to answer that question the way I'd like to."

Thank you counts!

EMAILS

Emails are a great way to follow up with someone who interviewed you. I recommend an email that thanks the person for their time, reiterates your desire to work for the company after having met the hiring manager and learned more about the company, and that uses a specific reference to a point in the conversation that was meaningful. Also, mention what you think sets you apart from the rest of the candidates. This lets the interviewer know you were paying attention, engaged, and that you strongly want to be a part of the company and the team.

THANK-YOU CARD

Personalized thank-you cards can really set you apart from the general population. They take a certain level of thoughtfulness, preparation, and effort that is appreciated. Plus, they are warmer and more personal than an email. Thank-you cards are appropriate for an acquaintance that you knew before the interview, such as the friend of a parent or other relative, a former classmate or teacher, or someone that you met personally who recruited you to apply for the job. You can send a thank-you card to the manager who interviewed you, or to a team or committee that sat down with you to ask you questions.

Other considerations:
- Do you have their address?
- Is it appropriate to get it?
- Can they receive mail at work?

Never ask someone for their home address to send a thank-you card. It crosses professional boundaries.

PHONE CALL

Phone calls are another good way to follow up. Sometimes, you will get an answering service or a mailbox; leave a pleasant message stating your name, the position you interviewed for, your interest in the company and the work, and a few qualities that set you apart from other candidates. Be sure to say thank you at the end of your message, and leave your full name and contact information.

If you do get the person who interviewed you on the line, be sure to be thoughtful of their time. Remember, your goal is to provide value and make the manager's life easier by being on their team, not harder. If you are going to make a phone call, I suggest the following:

Have a pen and paper handy, along with several prepared notes.

Introduce yourself again, and politely incorporate some of the particulars of the interview so that the person remembers you.

State the purpose of your call, and write down any information the interviewer tells you. (If they say decisions are being made within two weeks, don't bother them before that date asking if you got the job, etc.)

Thank the person for their time, and immediately follow any recommendations the person gives you.

Here's an example of a pleasant conversation. (These are imaginary people.)

"Hello, Ms. Bates? This is Samantha Bowers. I had the opportunity to meet with you on Thursday about staffing your retail storefront over the holidays."

"Ah, yes. How are you?"

"I'm doing great, thanks! I wanted to call and reiterate my interest in the position. I know you are looking for someone with open availability, and my schedule is very flexible. I'm a team player as well, and am happy to cover shifts, even at the last minute. I hope I am in your list of people being considered for this position, and would be happy to provide you with other references or letters of recommendation if you would find that valuable."

"Well, Samantha, I appreciate your call. We haven't made our final hiring decisions yet, but plan to do so by the end of the week. We will reach out through email and invite you to accept the position if the team decides to hire you."

"Thanks, Ms. Bates! I've got that written down on my calendar, and look forward to hearing from you soon. Thanks for taking the time to chat with me today!"

"You're welcome. Have a great day."

"You as well!"

The benefit of a follow-up email, card, or phone call is that it gives you a second opportunity to make your impression on the person who is in charge of hiring.

When they go down the list of names or when they revisit the applications, they will have seen/heard yours at least twice. They also will recognize that you made an extra effort **before** you had sealed the deal; they will expect to see that same type of character on the job when it comes to follow-through and going the extra mile.

They are likely to have a more pleasant feeling toward you, knowing that you went out of your way to appreciate their time; hiring managers conduct a lot of interviews, and they can be taxing, especially in positions with high turnover rates, such as retail and food and beverage industries.

Once you get your job, be the person you promised to be.

Arrive early, be aware of your environment, and go the extra mile to do the little things:

- Pick up the piece of trash on the floor
- Change the toilet paper when it is empty
- Wipe up spills
- Close the lid on the disinfecting wipes
- Organize the drawer properly
- Put things where they belong every time
- Make sure all the dollar bills are facing the same direction
- Wipe the glass

YOU CAN TEACH SKILLS TO ALMOST ANYONE
BUT
CHARACTER IS A WHOLE DIFFERENT STORY

In essence, do things that make life easier for everyone around you. Your managers will notice. Even if you're not rewarded for it in your first job—which you probably won't be—think of it this way: <u>you are getting paid to form and practice habits that make you a better employee, roommate, and partner.</u>

At some point, these habits will become a part of *who you are*, and when that happens, you will be able to grow in other areas. But, until you can be this kind of a team player, this kind of an employee and co-worker, the other skills won't matter, because you will be impossible to work with.

Ultimately, laziness and selfishness keep qualified people out of jobs. As an employer, you can teach skills to almost anyone; character is a whole different story.

When Is It Enough?

You will never have access to enough money to solve all of the world's problems. This is true with other finite goods as well. There will always be someone else who needs help, money, time, energy, or emotional support. You can't do it all. The first thing you must learn when it comes to being a money manager is boundaries. There is a book called *Boundaries* by Henry Cloud and John Townsend. Read the book!

You are going to have to say *NO*. No to yourself, no to your friends, no to your loved ones. You are going to have to say no to your wants, no to distractions, and no to anything that doesn't help you reach your goals.

Sometimes, you are going to have to put certain *needs* on hold and make compromises. Because you can't have everything you *need* and everything you *want RIGHT NOW*. That is a **cumulative** experience. That means you have to build up to it.

Prioritizing is important, and you have to line up each individual decision with a general, overall goal. You have to be ruthless in making choices about finances, because otherwise, they will storm the castle of your wellbeing and overthrow you completely.

Some Situations Where I can Practice My *No*

This space is for you to draw a picture about what saying "no" feels like to you. Are you empowered? Nervous? Embarrassed? Relieved? These are a variety of common responses. You're in good company!

There are always emergencies that come up, and you should just count on them. Erika Estrada, a Family and Consumer Science educator says:

> *"You can count on an emergency every six months. Know that it's coming, and recognize it for what it is when it shows up on your doorstep."*
>
> *—Erika Estrada*

Implied in that is that if you haven't had a recent emergency, you're about due for one! So be prepared for it!

Of course, it's more fun to buy a new dress than to spend $50 changing the oil in your car.

If you've been saving up for a new computer, but find out you have threadbare tires, what are you going to do?

It's really frustrating when your energy bill is $100 more than you expected, or when your coffee spills on your computer charger and it's an eighty-dollar oopsy.

But, here's a secret. **These kinds of things happen to everyone.** They derail everyone, except the people who are prepared for them. This next part about budgeting is going to help you prepare!

Let's Talk About Budgets

As soon as you get a job, it's important to budget your money. The following is not a good budget:

$20 Savings

$60 Phone bill

$40 Gas

$?? Whatever I want!

You need to see some percentages. If you're bringing home $450/month at a part time job, a $60 phone bill is approximately 13% of your income. Let's talk about what it means to "bring home" $450/month.

Your paycheck is your net income.

> **Net Income (take home money) =**
>
> Gross wages   [(the hours you work) x (hourly wage)]
>
> **MINUS**
>
> Taxes—Federal and State (anywhere from 10% to 23% for someone making minimum wage)
>
> **MINUS**
>
> Social Security and Medicaid Tax (7.65% of your gross wages)

If you make federal minimum wage, you will need to work roughly **20 hours per week** to bring home $450/month. By the time taxes, Social Security, and Medicaid are taken out of your check, you make roughly $5.60 per hour (if state and federal tax combined are 15%. That's an average, not the rule. Each state has a different tax percentage, from 0% to over 13%). That means: you work ten hours and forty-five minutes **per month** to pay your phone bill at $60 per month. That

$8 burrito you just ate? You worked one hour and twenty-five minutes for it.

You worked 37.5 minutes of clocked-in time to buy a $3.50 ice cream cone or equivalent snack.

Taking someone on a date and want to pick up the tab? Movies plus popcorn and a drink for two can easily run upwards of $40. That's **seven hours and eight minutes of work** for someone getting paid minimum wage. That doesn't count the cost of transportation to get to work, time spent getting ready, or the time on your commute!

So, what should you be spending your hard-earned money on?

Spend your money on investments that will help you make a better wage, and ultimately raise your quality of life.

INVESTMENTS LOOK LIKE...

BIKE

CAR

COMPUTER

WORKSHOPS

INTERVIEW CLOTHES

GAS/TRANSPORTATION

COSTS LOOK LIKE...

FOOD

SHOES

GAMES

MOVIES

DATE NIGHT

NAILS/HAIRCUTS

What are some of these investments?

Anything that is going to help you take the next step, achieve your next goal, or meet people who can mentor you gets to count as an investment.

Let's look at a good budget for that part-time job you're working; then we'll see what's missing and how we can boost it with a good use of time, energy, and resources.

Example Budget

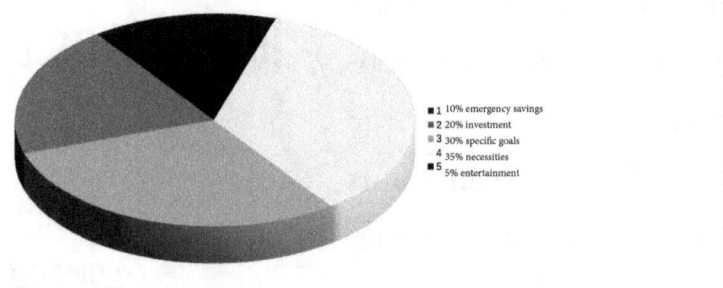

Gross Income: $580
Net Income: $450

($45) emergency savings
($90) investment
($135) specific goals
($157) necessities
($22) entertainment

Does this seem harsh? Maybe you are thinking, "Yeah, right. I'm a kid. I didn't get a JOB while I'm in school just to start spending all of my hard-earned money on stuff like that!"

It's tempting to buy a new pair of the latest basketball shoes, or something for entertainment like a Playstation or a big-screen TV. You're not alone. This is a temptation *everyone* faces, adults too!

There are ways you can reward yourself by putting aside money to get those

Example Budget

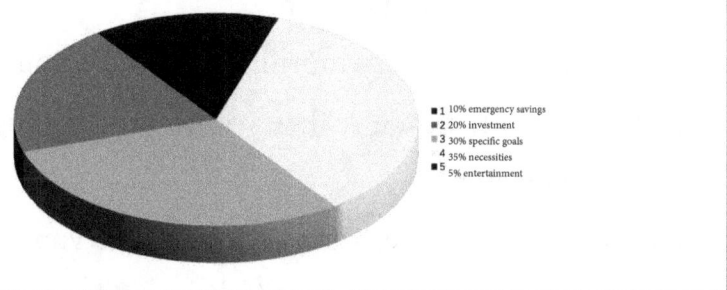

Gross Income: $580
Net Income: $450

($45) emergency savings
($90) investment
($135) specific goals
(~~$157~~) necessities
$147
(~~$22~~) entertainment
$10

things. Here's an example of how saving a few dollars here and there can make a difference. Let's take a look at this example month. You had $22 to spend on entertainment, but you pared down your spending.

You only spent $10 on entertainment because you met your friend for coffee rather than for dinner for a grand total of $5 (or 1 hour and 7 minutes of work). You spent $5 at the discount movie theater (some theaters have half-price day or discounts on the first showing of the day), and you didn't purchase snacks.

By making two good choices, you saved: $12!

You had to get shampoo ($8), facewash ($5), and a gym bag ($25 because you got it from Ross rather than at the Nike store) this month, on top of spending $60 on gas! With that $98 spent, you opted for a pack of granola bars as snacks ($6) rather than the more expensive beef jerky.

You filled up your water bottle every morning and saved yourself about twelve bucks this month that you didn't even realize you were spending on soda, sports drinks, and *gasp* bottled water.

You had to pay ($3) to enter the basketball game at your school since you forgot your ID, and you had to pay your car insurance ($40), which is under your parents' name and has a good student discount! (It's hard to spend money insuring the 1997 Ford Taurus. However, it gets you from A to B, and besides, you're saving up for a better car as you go!)

That is $147 spent out of your necessities budget!

"No way!" you think. "I didn't even GET that much." It's true. I double checked. But, feel free to do the math for yourself.

On a good note, you were $10 under budget in this category. Between that and the $12 you saved, you've now doubled your *disposable income* for February. See how this works?

Let's Crush Some of Your Best Arguments. Bring 'em On.

> I don't earn enough to put 20% toward "investment."

> $135 is too much to save every month for specific goals. $50 is more reasonable.

> My parents pay for my necessities. That whole $157 can go toward disposable income for me.

> You're crazy. I can't work twenty hours a week to only have $22 to spend on what I want. I quit.

I knew you weren't done! Go ahead. Write down some more moving arguments! Air it all out, right here.

I don't need an emergency fund.

You're totally right.

You don't need it.

Until you do. Then, you'll be very glad you have it.

Besides, if you save $45/month, that's only $540/year. It's not much, but it's a cushion. Here's a look at some things $540 will and will not do for you.

<u>NO</u>	<u>YES</u>
• It won't replace an iPhone ($600-$1,150).	• But, it will cover a trip to the doctor and antibiotics or necessary medication ($80-$130).
• It won't fix a transmission gone bad or a blown head gasket in your car ($1,000-$2,000).	• It will cover a headlamp for your car ($40-$80).
• It won't even pay for a trip to the ER in an ambulance (which costs anywhere from $600-$1,000).	• It should be enough to pay for a speeding ticket under most conditions ($150-$200).

By the way, that last one is one I hope you never get. A $150 speeding ticket is the equivalent of *26 hours and 45 minutes* at your minimum wage job.

The moral of the story is...

Carefully weigh the facts before speeding. If you are going to be more than 27 hours late, you should consider speeding. (That's a joke. It's sarcasm. The point is, speeding never makes sense. It saves you a few minutes, at most, and can cost you so much more, both financially and risk-wise.)

I don't earn enough to put 20% toward "investment."

The earning snowball

If you don't invest in yourself, in your skills, and in your education, you're going to be making minimum wage for a long, long time. The concept of "investment" implies that the money you put into it grows, and produces an outcome that is worth more over time.

Investment Cost

Cosmetology Education Cost $5,000-$15,000
Mechanic Education $10,000-$25,000
Associate Degree at Community College $8,000-$12,000
Bachelor Degree at State University (in-state tuition) $40,000-$60,000

Investment Benefit: Bigger Paychecks

High School Diploma	+ $203
Associate Degree	+ $288
Bachelor Degree	+ $661
Graduate Degree	+ $941

per week!

(compared with average wages of workers with no high school diploma)
U.S. Bureau of Labor Statistics, 2016

> "Full-time workers age 25 and older without a high school diploma had median weekly earnings of $494 in the first quarter of 2016. That compares with a median of $679 for high school graduates who never attended college and $782 for workers with some college or an associate degree. Median weekly earnings were $1,155 for workers with a bachelor's degree and $1,435 for workers with an advanced degree—a master's, professional, or doctoral degree." —U.S. Bureau of Labor Statistics

All of these educational programs that teach specific skills cost a lot of money. Start saving now, because no one wants to make $494 per week for the rest of his/her life. (Look up)

$135 is too much to put toward specific goals.

Let's take a look at some specific goals and see if we are out of line for saving 30% of monthly income to put toward these goals:

- Car
- Bike
- Plane ticket
- Laptop computer
- Securing an apartment (first and last month's rent plus deposit)
- Oil change
- New tires
- Wardrobe upgrades
- New phone (every two years)

_____

_____

_____

_____

Hmmm... I bet there is more than one thing on that list that appeals to you! Our goal with this particular fund is to always have some money in it. For example, if you spend $70 out of this fund the first month for a used bike that will help you get to your job, great! You now have $65 left in the fund to put toward something more expensive.

To put some of these things in perspective, let's look at pricing.

Car -driveable, usable, not fancy

Ex: 2014 Toyota Corolla basic package 56,000 miles is going to run you around $11,000 from the dealer.

Start saving now, and think about buying a good used "beater" from someone who is upgrading, at least until you can afford something more! Always do your due diligence! Check Kelly Bluebook for pricing particulars.

Bike - used $40-$70

Laptop computer - $300-$1800

Domestic flight - $100-$700 depending on season and availability

Apartment down payment (first and last month's rent) - $1,400 (this is not for some fancy high-rise!) In some places, $700 per month is a deal! This varies a lot from city to city. Ask your parents, relatives, and friends what they pay. Then, call a couple of real estate agencies or apartment locators in your area and ask them what they require for a first-time renter!

Oil Change - $40-$80

New Tires - $500-1,800 depending on the make and model of your vehicle

Wardrobe Upgrades - I personally think $25-$50 per month is sufficient to keep your wardrobe fresh and neat, but occasionally you will need shoes or particulars that are more expensive. A good idea is to shop used or discount stores.

New Phone - $300-$900 for a good smartphone

What else??

Put your money toward specific goals, rather than letting it slip through your fingers for frivolous things. **You can set your own specific goals**; however, make sure they are going to serve you well and that they are not simply consumer items that don't serve a meaningful purpose.

My parents pay for my necessities.

You lucky dawg! They've had to work very hard to be able to provide you with your lifestyle. But, one day, you will turn 18, become an adult, and they won't be paying your bills anymore.

Take advantage of this time, do a favor for your future self, and put that 35% right into investments and specific goals. Split it right down the middle. Reach your current goals faster, and help your future self reach your goals faster as well.

Plan well, and you will someday be able to provide this same type of support for someone you care about! And, thank your mom and dad, or whoever raises you, for their hard work, and the sacrifices they make so you can have a good life.

Take out the trash, unload the dishwasher, or offer to carry groceries in from the car. Show them how much they're appreciated. After all, they are saving you at least 28 hours at your minimum wage job every month. And that's not taking food or housing costs into consideration!

You're crazy. I can't work twenty hours a week to only have $22 a month to spend on what I want. I quit.

You can spend money on what you want! But it should work toward a goal rather than be frivolous and wasteful. The point is, *you* have to be able to support yourself one day, and now is the time to figure out your budget, find a way to purchase things that will make your life easier and open up your job options, (such as a car, a skill, a computer), and establish a savings fund so you aren't derailed by an emergency.

BEFORE MAKING ANY PURCHASE, MAKE SURE IT CORRESPONDS WITH YOUR GOALS

If you won't cut your entertainment budget, and you continue that habit, one day you will be cutting your food and heat budget to pay off your credit cards because you let money be your master. Learn the habit of restraint now. Allow there to be time between experiencing a want or need, and having it filled. Do it for three months. Can you?

> **Learn the habit of restraint now.**

After three months, evaluate what it feels like to have a few hundred dollars saved in your emergency and investment funds. Imagine what that would feel like if you had thousands, and if you had already paid for the education, investment, and you didn't have to worry about going broke over an emergency.

That's the person you can be, so let's get you there as soon as possible. If you start with this plan today, and stick with it, you'll feel like a real boss at twenty-five, not like some frivolous teenager who went broke over shoes or a purse or video games that will be turfed, scuffed, and outdated by the time you're twenty-five.

Some Special Situations Where it's Crucial to Have Your Finances Under Control

It's important to have the following things set up, and in working order:

- [ ] Uber app
- [ ] Lyft app
- [ ] $20 in your phone case as emergency money (such as for a taxi or gas)
- [ ] Emergency Contact in your phone
- [ ] Someone who knows where you are, and how long you plan to be there

---

Good talk.

Now, go handle the first three before you move on!

Don't turn that page. Not until you've resolved these three things!

In some phones, there is a place to add In Case of Emergency (ICE) contacts and information. This is nice because there is a place to add allergies, blood type etc. as well as key phone numbers of people to contact.

In most cases, this information is accessible from your phone, even if it is locked with a password.

If your phone doesn't have this capacity, save a couple of emergency contacts under ICE Mom, ICE Dad, ICE Brother, etc. Make sure your emergency contacts know the following crucial bits of information:

Birthdate

Any allergies

Blood type

Go ahead and shoot those people a text right now that includes that information. Simply say, "I've added you as an emergency contact. Please save the following information in your notes on your phone." Include the crucial bits of information and you're set!

No, really.
Just do it, please. Right now.

This next section deals with to some particular situations where having your money in order and being able to quickly access those funds comes into play. We will discuss travel, both domestic and international, parties, dates, and weekends away with friends.

All of these activities require that you spend money. Sometimes, young people spend all of their money on the event, and then don't have a cushion or any emergency money if things go wrong.

We are going to look at the basics of a backup plan so that you can enjoy these activities without putting yourself or others in danger, in trouble, or even just in an awkward situation that could have been avoided.

When traveling, you need to have the checklist from page 48 fully completed, set up, and verified **plus** *the following:*

- Debit or Credit Card with at least $700 available. If you need to get a hotel room and/or buy a flight home ASAP, you're going to need to access these funds in a hurry.
- Several photos of your ID or Passport:
    - One printed copy left with a trusted person who is not traveling
    - One photo emailed to yourself so you can access it from any computer
    - One photo saved to your phone and shared with your travel partner
- A spare credit card that is kept in a secure place that is **not** with any other cards; if you get robbed or lose your wallet/purse, this will be your go-to
- The names and phone numbers of trusted people at home in case of emergency
- The name, address, and phone number of your hotel (written in the country's language if you are traveling internationally)
- The address and phone number of the American Embassy in each country you are visiting when traveling abroad
- Register with the U.S. Embassy through the Smart Traveler Enrollment Program (STEP) before you go at https://step.state.gov/step/

The Big 3

ID

Access to Funds

Contacts

It's always hard to be pro-actively prepared. Sometimes, we have a tendency to get burnt a time or two before we cognitively recognize the benefits of planning ahead. It's important to understand that mistakes happen. You have to give yourself some grace as you try things out and learn from your mistakes.

True Story:

Once upon a time, I was in France, traveling with a group of students and various chaperones.

We were eating lunch outside the breathtaking Palace of Versailles, not far outside of Paris. It was a beautiful summer day, and in Europe, dining on the patio is a lovely experience.

Seated a couple of tables away from my group were some other members on our tour. One of the chaperones hung her purse on the back of her chair while she ate. By the time lunch was over, the purse was gone.

She had her purse snatched from right under her nose! Credit cards, cash that had been converted from dollars to euros, and her passport were all in the purse, in an easy get-one-get-all bundle for the thief to take.

She missed going to see the *Palais*, and instead, spent all day at the American Embassy trying to get a legitimate ID, and on the phone with her credit card companies trying to cancel the cards before the charges racked up. Multiple purchases had already been made by the time she contacted her card companies. That's a rough day in France!

There are some mistakes that are really hard to recover from, however. And these are mistakes you really don't want to make. At times, even when you make the best decisions, bad situations will happen to you. So, here are some examples of various situations that can develop. The goal is to help you be prepared so you can avoid some awful consequences. What would you do? Think about how you would handle the financial issues related to each scenario:

1. You're staying with a bunch of friends (at a sports tournament, a trip to Washington, D.C., a trip to Europe) and your roommate/friend ends up:
   - Making you uncomfortable
   - Bringing people you feel uncomfortable around into the room and won't make them leave
   - Bringing alcohol or illegal drugs into your room (in which case, should there be a bust, this could go on your record as a possession charge or worse)
   - You find out the people you traveled with have different motives than were stated and you want to go home
2. You find out a "business meeting" or "interview" was actually a lure by a person in power who wanted other types of favors from you
3. There is a family emergency that requires you to return home immediately

It's always best to be prepared. There's nothing like being stuck someplace where you are uncomfortable (or with people you don't want to be with) because you don't have the money to get yourself out of it.

Being prepared lends you a sense of confidence as well, which makes predators less likely to bother you. It is people who come across as desperate or without options who make the best targets.

I'm not saying you can't still experience bad things or bad people even if you do all the proactive, well-prepared decision-making possible; I'm just saying to make it as unlikely as possible by having all your options and resources at your fingertips.

Bonus Warnings: Parties and Dates

There are two situations that are cause for great concern when it comes to young people: parties and dates. Both of these situations can be a lot of good, clean fun, but both also present great opportunities for things to go very wrong. Let's deal with two elephants in the room: accidents—particularly related to substance abuse—and rape. Both of these are major concerns at parties and on dates.

TABOO TOPICS

Dates

Parties

Accidents

Rapes

You should have the Uber/Lyft apps and a $20 bill with you at all times so that you are free to get out of any situation in which you find yourself.

If you are at a party, and the person you caught a ride with is drinking, excuse yourself to the bathroom and contact Uber or Lyft. Shoot your friend a text, and get them to go with you if possible. But whatever you do, don't get in a car with that person behind the wheel. Get their keys from them, and get alternate transportation.

If the party gets out of hand, or if someone makes you feel uncomfortable, just leave. Call Uber. There will be more parties and yes, you will get invited to them. But you only have one life. Protect it, and be smart.

The same goes for dates. Never put your well-being into the hands of someone who hasn't earned your trust. Note that I said *EARNED*. We just got done talking about money and value. Trust over your drink, your body, or your life shouldn't be tossed around. Make those people **earn** your trust every step of the way.

We've all seen the movies where somebody gets a little too handsy on a first date (or a second, third, etc.). Unfortunately, as a society we have been desensitized to these negative types of behavior. That means we have seen them so much, they seem almost normal. **It's not normal!**

THE GIFT OF FEAR
Gavin de Becker

If you want more information on domestic violence, dangerous stalking situations, red flags by people in general, and how to manage yourself and make decisions in bad circumstances, this book is a must read.

A word of caution: if whoever you are dating doesn't respect your "no," GET OUT! Some people will push your boundaries and at some point, they may cross them. Make sure you are prepared to pay your tab and find your own way home if a date goes sour.

Don't laugh off any indecencies, or let someone make you feel like a prude if you aren't comfortable with the way they are acting. You should only have to say something once. If they don't respect your boundary, don't stay there. It is better to be "rude" and not finish the date than to allow someone to make you uncomfortable and risk undesirable consequences.

What if they don't respect boundaries and "no"s?

This is where you have to make a judgment call. You can say, "I appreciate your time, but I'm done with this date." Get up from the table, approach your server (if at a restaurant) to pay your tab, and leave (call an Uber if you were picked up or dropped off).

If you don't feel comfortable saying that, or if you don't believe that the person is going to "let" you go, excuse yourself to the bathroom and request a Lyft. While you're in there, text a trusted parent, aunt, coach, or friend and let them know where you are and where you are headed with an estimated time of arrival. Let them know the full name of the person you were with, as well. This is just a good precaution. If you are doing any online dating, you should share this pertinent information with a trusted person before meeting someone for a date.

When your ride is outside, exit the restroom, pick up anything you left at the table (such as a coat; your personal belongings such as phones, wallets, and purses should be with you at all times!) and simply say, "Goodbye." The person might call out after you, using your name, or phrases like "I'm sorry."

Ignore them.

Keep on walking, head held high, and don't look down until you reach your ride. You must keep all your wits about you. Now, and only now, is the time to pull out your phone and finally block that person from your contacts! You can also send a text to the parent, aunt, friend, etc. and let them know you are safely in your Lyft and update them on the time of arrival.

Remember, **stick up for yourself!** Trust your gut. Even if everyone in your circle thinks you're weird, paranoid, or a drama queen, know that there are survivors of rape, attempted murder, accidents, and other tragedies who are applauding your courage. Take a stand for yourself.

Bonus Warnings: Roommates and Credit

Never live with your best friend until you're in your 30s.

The end.

Just kidding. There's more, although that's a solid piece of advice. The reason is because there have been too many friendships and too many bank accounts ruined by a lack of caution in choosing a roommate.

When you sign up to rent an apartment or a house, you are entering into a binding, legal contract. You sign your name on the line, and the person or company you are renting from has the right to hold you to your lease agreement, and pursue legal action if you don't.

LEASE AGREEMENT

Legal contract
Linked to your credit score
Can blacklist you if you break a lease
Can require a co-signer
Requires a deposit
Holds you accountable for damages

There are no extenuating circumstances that will get you out of this agreement. It doesn't matter if you lose your job, if you get mono, or if your mother dies. The legal agreement doesn't have *feelings*, and it doesn't care how much your life sucks right now.

It only cares about one thing: that you pay, and that you pay on time. (Remember that emergency fund you've been saving since you got that first job three years ago? Don't spend it. Keep adding to it in case your roommate goes crazy and you're stuck paying the whole lease on just your income.)

There's something REALLY special about signing a lease with someone. Not only do you get to arrange the living room and the kitchen cupboards together, but you also get to be held legally accountable for that person's lack of paying their half of the rent, should they decide to do so. When you sign a lease with someone, you're not only taking yourself on as a risk (What if I get hurt? Or lose my job? Or get into an accident and am hospitalized?), but you're taking on the same risks for the other person.

This whole "responsibility" thing is new to <u>EVERY</u> teenager who steps out on their own for the first time. And, guess what? Every person makes mistakes along the way. The goal here in choosing a roommate wisely is to mitigate as many of the potential risks and negative outcomes as possible.

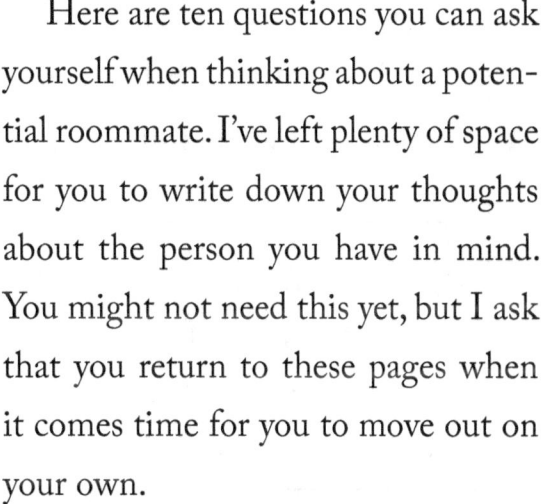

Keep it Real

Here are ten questions you can ask yourself when thinking about a potential roommate. I've left plenty of space for you to write down your thoughts about the person you have in mind. You might not need this yet, but I ask that you return to these pages when it comes time for you to move out on your own.

One other thing. Remember, this book is for you. These activities are for your benefit so that you can make the most informed decisions possible. So keep it real. Don't rush through these answers. Consider them. Process them. Practice what you would do in a given situation (remember Captain de Crespigny?)

It's always better to go into a situation with your eyes wide open. So, answer honestly, think of examples that demonstrate how this person's **behavior answers the questions**, make your decision, and then *prepare for what could happen*.

1. Is this person reliable? _____
   _____

2. Does this person have a job where they make enough money to pay their bills?_____
   _____

3. Is this person responsible? Does he/she show up on time to class and other functions?_____
   _____

4. Does this person have good communication skills? Can I disagree with this person without it blowing up into a big argument?_____
   _____
   _____

5. Does this person have good personal boundaries?_____
   _____
   _____

6. Does this person respect my boundaries?_____
   _____
   _____

7. Does this person have any habits that can potentially bother me or put me at risk? Smoking? Drinking? Drugs? Overnight guests? _____
   _____
   _____

8. Is this person good with their finances? Are they fair? Will it be a fight to get their share of the rent, utilities, Internet, etc.?_____

_____

_____

_____

9. Does this person have a healthy lifestyle? Are they tidy, or will I be the only person putting effort into having a clean home?_____

_____

_____

10. Does this person go out of their way to help? Can we have teamwork and communication on things such as meals, parking, and chores?_____

_____

_____

This is just the tip of the iceberg. However, I generally recommend that you NOT live with your best friend during your first endeavor of living on your own.

There is a lot of growth in that first year of being an adult, and I'd rather you not ruin your strongest relationship because of the difficult moments that bring that growth about. I see people take advantage of their friend, be judgmental, not deal with their new freedoms well, and ultimately resent the person they used to love the most.

It's not to say you can't ever live with your best friend; just get some practice under your belt with someone with whom you might have an easier time making and maintaining more clear-cut boundaries.

Set Boundaries!

The last part of this chapter is going to deal with all kinds of credit. Credit cards, student loans, and borrowing against your future paycheck.

It's true, modern society and economics have been built on these very habits. It is unreasonable to say "never get a credit card," or "don't take out any student loans."

That is, however, the best advice if you are not ABSOLUTELY **cutthroat** about dealing with your debt. Money management, time management, and self-discipline are very closely linked.

Go back to that concept of time spent at a job per buying power of the dollar.

Paper or Plastic?

$1 worth of buying power = 10 minutes and 45 seconds at work if you are paid minimum wage.

> ### Hint
>
> When researching for facts, try to use as many .gov and .edu sites as possible; this will guarantee a more reliable source

(This varies based on the state income tax; in some states there is no state income tax while in CA, it is upward of 13%. Federal tax for most people working a minimum wage job will be between 10-15% of their gross earnings. I have used 15% total tax as an example throughout this book. You can figure your state income tax by looking it up online.)

When you use credit, **you are borrowing from your future self**. For every dollar you spend on credit (that you don't have the money to pay back right away), you are likely to pay somewhere between 14%-22% interest yearly, called Annual Percentage Rate (APR).

It's important that you figure out exactly what the rules are with your particular credit card company, if you have one. Each card is different, each bank is different, and things like your credit score impact the particulars of your credit card.

It's okay to call and ask for specifics. Contact your credit card company and ask them to give you information about how your card works. Ask them to go over the interest rate (the APR), and how that translates on a **daily** basis.

Your credit card company will be happy to go over the specifics with you, and they will help you figure out when you need to pay your bill, and how you can pay your bill before interest is due.

Remember, in most situations, if you carry a balance on your credit card, you are going to pay interest on the amount that you owe. Each card is unique. Some have yearly fees; some have introductory APRs that change over time. The best thing you can do is educate yourself. Call the company and get specifics from them so you can make an educated decision.

> # HINT
> Most people make bad decisions in the heat of the moment. You can overcome this by making a plan before you end up in that situation! Decide what you are going to do in a non-emotional time, then stick to your guns!

Decide what your list of expectations looks like. Here is an example of some restrictions and boundaries someone who is trying to avoid paying a lot of interest might create:

<u>**NO**</u>	<u>**YES**</u>
• Don't treat your friends to coffee or pick up someone's tab at lunch. (Exceptions would be when you have planned that in or budgeted it for a special occasion, like a birthday.)	• Leave your credit card at home, when possible. If you don't have it on you, you can't borrow from it!
• Don't buy perishable things like snacks, gum, or sports drinks on credit.	• Set a spending limit and only use the card for special things that you have predetermined you were going to buy.
• Don't have your card on you when you stop by the mall or the bookstore.	• Pay it off ON TIME every month. You are likely to get dinged a hefty fee if you are even a day late!
• _____	• _____
• _____	• _____
	• _____

Another way that some people borrow money is through payday advance loans or through pawn shops. It is important to know what the stipulations of repayment are before you enter into any financial agreement. Ask what the interest rate is, and when you will need to pay back the loan.

Feel free to ask the person who is helping you to run the numbers for you. They might be able to tell you not only the interest rate, but also the exact amount of money you will have to pay back by a certain date.

You can then compare the amount you owe with the amount you are borrowing and decide for yourself if you are willing to pay the rate they are charging.

Interest on credit starts to add up very quickly. Many of us have gotten ourselves into a position where it is almost impossible to pay the debt off for two reasons:

1. We couldn't afford it in the first place—and not a lot changed between last month's bills and this month's bills.
2. We can't keep up with the interest payments!

It snowballs. The **bigger** the original debt, the **faster** that number grows. Only you can decide how much you are going to spend and how much you can afford. Consider the cost before you make the purchase.

If you discover that you are borrowing more than you can afford, you might want to seek some professional financial help. It's better to make a plan as soon as possible so that you don't get in over your head!

The Skinny on Student Loans

Sometimes, people choose to take out student loans when they attend college or a trade school. Remember, if you choose to take out a loan, you are agreeing to make sure your future self pays it.

Borrowing money is, in some situations, a necessary and helpful hand up. As with any borrowing, there is risk involved because no one can predict what their grades will be, or what kind of a job they are going to get. Many schools offer counseling and information sessions on borrowing so that you can be better informed before you make the decision to borrow. Attend these sessions, ask questions, and really evaluate how much you **need** before you take out the loan.

It is a great idea to find a part-time job, even while you are in school, to help offset some of the costs of your education. Sometimes there are work-study programs at your school that allow you to work around your class schedule. Jobs that have evening availability might be a good fit if most of your classes are in the morning. Remember, every dollar you earn and put toward your investment today is a dollar that you won't have to pay interest on in the future.

It's important to find a few people that you trust and who are *fiscally responsible* with whom you can have conversations regarding money. Don't ask the broke guy down the street or the relative who is always trying to get out of a jam. Ask people who are where you want to be. Talk to people who live a modest lifestyle, but who always manage to have something to give.

They may not be the folks with the fanciest car, the newest shoes, or the nicest house, because many of those people are in debt up to their ears and are suffering greatly due to their lifestyle choices.

Remember: *flash* and *cash* rarely go together. Seriously. Do the research. Check out how many big lottery winners, major athletes, and former movie stars go broke.

It's not always about how much money you make, but how you manage that money, *especially* when it comes to credit, debt, and loans with interest.

Congratulations!

You finished the first part of this course, and you are well on your way to establishing your M in your MICCC!

Here are a few other things for you to revisit as you finish up this section:

- What are some of my major weaknesses that would keep someone from hiring me?
- How can I work on them? Who can I trust to help me work on them?

- Do I plan to go to college? When and where? Could I go to community college for the first two years to save myself some major money?

- What are my specific qualities that will make me a good employee?

- What are my investment ideas and opportunities?

- What are some special goals for which I would like to set aside money?

- What organizations can I join to get some experience for my resumé?

- Where are the three biggest areas where I waste time on a daily basis. Can I reduce that by one-third? What can I do that is productive and that puts me on the path to my goals during the time that I have saved?

- What are some things I'm looking forward to when I get more independence? What are some of the responsibilities I'm going to face when I have that independence? Am I prepared for all of those things at once? How can I start taking more independent responsibility so that I am gaining that confidence and capability while I'm still getting help from my parents?

- What is my work availability?

- Where are five places I'd like to work and why?

- What will I plan to do while I'm studying my career path in order to make a living?

- What does my budget look like?

- Do I know five people who will write me a letter of recommendation?

Follow the principles in this book, and you will be so far ahead of the person you would have been if you hadn't fought through some of these concepts now, before making potential mistakes!

What if I've Already Ruined my Chances?

If you're reading this book and you've already completely messed up and ruined your finances, your credit, your relationships, and your work history, take heart. It will be a long path to climb out of the hole you've dug, but it is doable. You have to start! And now is better than a day later.

You might need to get some expert counseling from someone who can help you in your specific situation. If you don't have a job, get one! There are temp agencies, restaurants who need dishwashers, and hotels that need cleaned. If you have an arrest, don't lose heart! There are jobs available for you! Check out www.jobsforfelons.org, or speak with a small business owner with whom you already have a relationship.

Get out there, and start earning an income. Be judicious about how you spend your money. You are going to be very tired, more tired than you've ever been. That's because your past self put you in this situation. There is no way around it, only through it.

Learn the value of HARD work. Master yourself. Be ruthless in what you spend your money on. Beans and rice will take you a long way.

Do everything you must do to set yourself free from your debts. Don't look up until you come through the other side. When you do, you will have a renewed sense of confidence and belief in yourself that no one can take away. And you will have earned the badge of knowing you have mastered self!

ACKNOWLEDGMENTS

This book is in your hands because of the collaborative efforts of many special people who have read it, shared their opinions and comments, and made it approachable for many diverse readers.

First thanks goes to Denya Jacobs, who has faithfully encouraged my writing and my public speaking. Without her, neither my TEDxPlano Talk nor the "Bring Your MICCC" speech that inspired the book would exist. You inspire me to push my limits. Thank you.

A special thanks to Erika Vargas Estrada for the hours spent on the topics of social change, making a difference, and education; thank you for carefully pondering the content in this book, and for helping me make it better. Most importantly, thank you for coming up with the "C" for curiosity! This has been influential in my life, as well as in the production of the *Bring Your MICCC* series.

Thanks to Erin Huebener, a thousand times! I appreciate your keen eye for both content and details, your ability to point out flaws and your counsel on how to make projects better. Most of all, I'm thankful for your good, solid sense, and your enduring patience with me! Thank you for allowing me to stay in your home while I wrote this book; thank you for encouraging me to leave the basement and do other things, such as go outside, walk the dogs, hit the gym, and eat.

Thank you, Vanessa Flores, for your tireless efforts on getting a great cover for the *Bring Your MICCC* series! Your enthusiasm, coachability, and work ethic are a great example of the principles stated in this book, and you handle your many responsibilities with such poise. You go, girl.

Aunt Cherie, thank you for the wonderful line edits you provided! You helped me burn the chaff in this book and produce the best product possible. Much love!

Thank you, Mark Schultz, AKA Word Refiner, for your careful attention to detail and for your precise spelling-editing. Your recommendations are always phenomenal! Thank you for making this book better.

Thank you, Joshua Hill, for putting together the music and capturing the audio for the trailer for this book. You work so hard, and you are an inspiration.

Thanks to the wonderful folks who let me interview them and get their insights! Andy Brown, Caroline Bickford, and Robert Jones—your lives speak to the MICCC that you have developed. Thank you for sharing your thoughts.

A huge shout of gratitude to the most amazing launch team. Thanks for being one hundred percent behind this project and working under tight deadlines! The success of this book is completely due to your efforts, collaboration, and the momentum you build. Caroline Bickford, Andy Brown, Cory Cooper, Erika Vargas Estrada, Cherie Ferguson, Mary-Ellen Gomez, Robert Jones, Lauren Klemke, Raziel Leiva, Erick Locker, Mike Scott, Mark Schultz, Amber Steinborn, Katie Towers, and Mark Wilson.

Thanks to my mom and dad, who taught me that I had a voice, and that my opinion was valuable. I started developing my MICCC around our kitchen table when I was just a child. Mom, I miss you. You would have loved this.

A special thanks to my sister, Lori, who is always happy to read my first drafts, give feedback, and encourage me to finish the project!

Thank you, my wonderful brother Matt, for your constant encouragement, for constantly coaching me throughout the years, and for always being there to help.

Thank you, Bear, for your friendship, encouragement, and everlasting belief in me. Thank you for valuing my voice, and for being my hero and mentor in so many ways.

To all of my friends and colleagues, and to everyone who liked, shared, and recommended this book to others, thank you for your amazing support of this project. Together, we can make a difference!

To all of the young people who have read this book and implemented growth and coachability into your lives, thank you. Thank you for believing in yourselves and for taking the time to start with yourself. You can change the world.

BIBLIOGRAPHY

Duhigg, Charles. *Smarter Faster Better* Random House, 2016.

Hughes, Tony J. "What Air Crash Investigations Didn't Tell You About QF32 (Airbus A380)." *LinkedIn,* 26 Dec, 2014, https://www.linkedin.com/pulse/what-air-crash-investigations-didnt-tell-you-qf32-airbus-hughes/. Accessed 10 Jan, 2018.

Cuddy, Amy. "Your Body Language May Shape Who You Are." *TED Global*, June 2012, https://www.ted.com/talks/amy_cuddy_your_body_language_shapes_who_you_are.

Bureau of Labor Statistics. United State Department of Labor, 11 May 2016, https://www.bls.gov/opub/ted/2016/weekly-earnings-by-educational-attainment-in-first-quarter-2016.htm. Accessed 7 Jan, 2018.

"Money." *Mirriam-Webster Online Dictionary,* 2018, https://www.merriam-webster.com. Accessed 10 Jan, 2018.

www.ingramcontent.com/pod-product-compliance
Lightning Source LLC
Chambersburg PA
CBHW060457300426
44113CB00016B/2630